anime

animus

anima

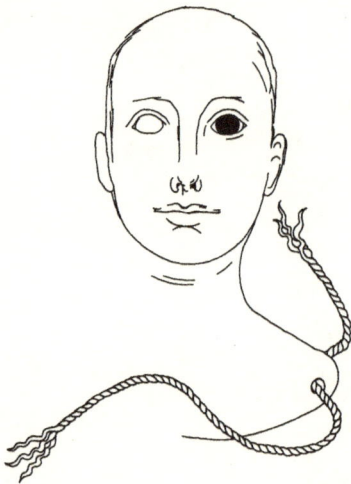

anime
animus
anima

jaime robles

○

shearsman books
2010

First published in the United Kingdom
in 2010 by
Shearsman Books Ltd.
54 Velwell Road
Exeter EX 4 4 LD
www.shearsman.com

ISBN 978-1-84861-088-0
FIRST EDITION

Cover image copyright © Janne Ahvo, 2008
Book design and illustrations by Jaime Robles
Author photo: Irene Young

contents

one: black

two: white

three: color

11

Distinguishing the virtual from the real is a major error on the part of human beings. To me, the birth and death of a human being is already a virtual event.

—MAMORU OSHII

If our Gods and our hopes are nothing but scientific phenomena, then let us admit it must be said that our love is scientific as well.

—AUGUSTE VILLIERS DE L'ISLE-ADAM
Tomorrow's Eve, 1886

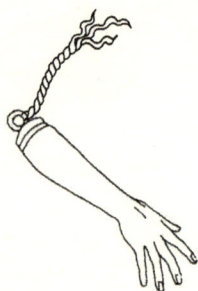

000000001

black

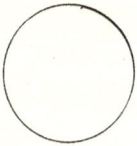

in the theater's darkened hollow
the film flutters—

fissure through which
we swim, inchoate

blackened

facing
surface bright
in patches and streaks: thin skin
where eyes see, ears hear,
but the mouth—its voice—
gathers silence

splash of green
yellow fizz

blue wash above

along	the
black	strip
between	frames
where	projected
light	neither
permeates	nor
reflects:	distance
and	time
congeal.	The
eye	leaps
through	unexposed
blackness,	resolves
solid	gesture
into	solid
gesture	24
times	faster
than	a
blink.	Eye
shudders	into
movement.	The
body	— the
ship —	leaps
through	vast
circles.	Within
each	sphere
space	dissolves
ticking	and
eye	records
a	downpour
of	particles.
Behind	eye
and	body
our	mind
stumbles	to its
own	metronome,
memory	releases
and	we
fly	here
and	now

Placid sky and distant on a cloudless day

What is projected before us is not photographic:

> pigment suspended, veiling
> the wall in memory

> —images archive
> freeze time

> lack words' metamorphic thought

> everything appears a bordered field of color

oo

A blink shuttered

fractured second—in daylight—

        caught open: the wide eye a path

Nor is the eye a camera:

As she falls backwards out the window, she disappears:

fading   cat like,

smile

    body:

        dropping
        into flight in silence

        through night
        falling into place before
        the city's neon. Skyscrapers

        cascade speckled with lumens,
        tubular as arteries.

Perhaps she hasn't fallen at all

Rather: the buildings risen
in urgent growth
dragging behind them earth
and human floor.

oo

soul:

    glimmering particle

  in the brain—

     a glassy sliver

the body:

layer by layer

dipped

waxy, nubile, weightless

the womb
vegetable and liquid:

outer skin peels, fragments float upward
rain down, lack of odor prevails
over the smell of blood—

a chorus of women's voices chimes
deep in the chest

and the optometrist, who is a man,
turns the lens over:
Do the letters on the green square look blacker now
—flips the lens—

or now?

Now, or now ...

now, or now?

oo

It is not the body's perimeter that is unimaginable but its surface. He wraps her glowing curves into his jacket, and will repeat the gesture as often as he feels necessary. Her skin draws a third side to his love, impossible but accommodating. Doll-like, her body—torso and limbs—are exchangeable: only her eyes—the blue lens, slick, dilating—and that slice of mind, the recollection of her past, irretrievable. He will swap that body as the flesh fails. For her, there is no difference between the skin she claims her own and air

∞

Light divides with a scalpel's flash into seconds or moments:

everything translates simultaneously:

east into north, north into wooden chair,
chair into green grapes, grapes into whirr, whirr into
wreathes of cypress, cypress (*cypress*) into salt:

tying breath to breath

an ocean into light-splashed face

Key Animator

an instant's curves
spill from a young man's
hand. For him

        soul:
                is body—

                under whose twin moons
                he sways drunken, silly,

                in time
                to antique words

beautiful dreamer

        the body:

                exquisite

                spent cartridge

                an oblong of light fallen on black linoleum

rings of the shining moon

and letters pinned to the page

The body's curves
sweep from the pen's oblong point,

Lines razor diagrams between one color and another, balloon
into volume:

                        because

                        the body

                        contains

                        no gradations

                        only slopes—

                        foreground/background

                        wheel and cog

at the nape of her neck

    nobbed stairway to the head: thought: soul

        where the hair
        tumbles
        parts
        in lank cascades

the kimono falls away
depicts its own exact
arc

        apart:
        thin wires connect us
        to each other's voices

        parades of light
        radiate information like a teeming city—

        netted,

        minus the body's
        neural lattice

wash of color
lit interior

smoke lifting through aloof sky

oo

In the vast vastness of space you cannot
escape isolation: proximate and contiguous;
sizzle of an air filtration system, background
jazz bleeding into awareness. Not here
in the midst of freeway congestion, dust
trembling, accidental accumulations:

counting things and more things, pages in books read,
and counting the un-read until you and I are cloaked.

                                        Unmerged
space sheds us, chartreuse feathers spin
through gravity until time
stills—riffled, not shuffled like a deck of new cards

— I will wait for you, my love, until this clock runs down.

oo

Life, shaved, bedizened,
overrides the baked landscape of words—
no pause buttoned into the flow

At any moment
we will leave
for the lobby
outside—

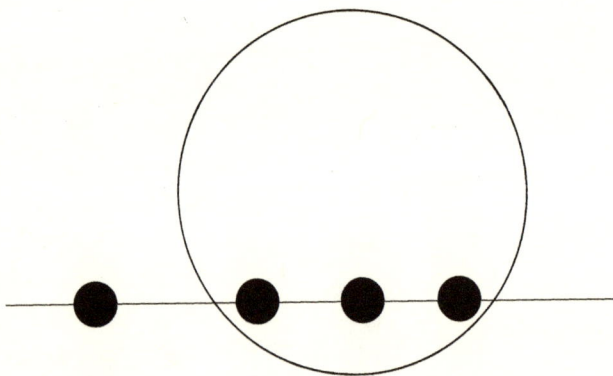

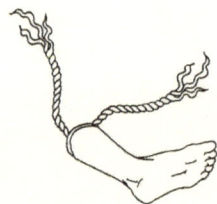

OOOOOOOO10

white

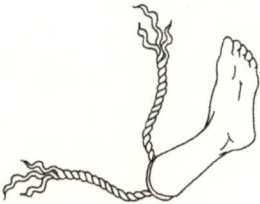

An eye is a hole through which the world enters …
Place it between the legs and, there, the image
is no longer in focus, instead is a fluctuation:
flickering and animal, entering
the body like a periscope to examine
the heart sheathed in a lavish of ribs.
What does the heart know of the eye's image
tracked down in chiaroscuro?
They face each other: heart,
avian and buoyed by air, reformed by eye into
a raven, towhee, stellar jay, acrobatic swallow,
a rage of categories slung into the air like a boomerang.
In the background the sun winces down
on a broken picnic table, calligraphic

oo

In the vessel of memory, mother is a field
with pastel sky and green cascades, vibrating
between hues: shade
and starry celestial light.

She was a place of containment.
But mother—brilliant as always—stepped through: divested
herself of ego: married her flesh to metal
and some monstrous concept.

The child simmers his memory:
fermenting mother and moments
into rich food

∞

Can a stitch in time sew up
a tear in space, pulling
four dimensions into three?
Or two? Thread's
slim line follows transparent needle
curves in tight around the edges—
seaming nothingness
into space
colorless and shimmering as silk.
A stab of pain catches the breath:
thumb pricked, a globe
of red wobbly at the tip

The brain is the heart

When the child is wrapped
into this machine,
absorbed,
subsumed,
it is the brain
that motivates,
directs, breathes,
runs, fights

Isn't it?

Polyflamed surge:

molecular flood—

charged—

macaronic—

That child is no longer human.
That machine is no more—

No
more

And heart is
no more than
brain,

is it

Unsalvageable

Through waters gone catastrophic she coasts,
saved like a pickle in a jar:
her capsule the home where all children capable of destruction
and rescue are encased, where they mend nervous
impulse into armored monster—

Red, red, crimson lake …

When she lands at last she's an orphan:
escapee from racing clouds, coiled inward, formed into something
like a woman's torso: undecided: expellant and containing death.

Scarlet sky, russet land, crimson waves—red, red   red …

Mother, again, is missing.
What choice did she make?

oo

A girl enters an elevator to find another girl
within. The elevator floats above silence,
following gravity's urge, forming a bubble in time.
She faces east, she faces south:
She blinks, or perhaps that was only you, the watcher.
Seconds pass. Hmmmmmmmm. Doors open,
escalators carry figures down, and down:
Song takes place elsewhere—in the corridor between opposites.

A woman sits facing elsewhere, only the light flickers:
she confesses that there are long landscapes,
narrow spaces between immense ceilings and floors stretched out,
reflecting silhouettes—both floor and ceiling red,
etched with mystical figures, multiple angel wings—
where no one moves.

Cast out to sea

(the imagination of free will + memory) equals self
divided from others but not minus matter …

self slithers across thought …

And mother equals zero, which is indivisible
from the self, which is one, and the other, which is 2.
Or any other number because $n = n + 0$ as
$a = a$

Or minus A equals A times—which is the opposite
of divided by (but in this case the results
are the same)—minus one.

Which is to say A times minus one equals A divided
by minus one,

as surely as mother $= 0$

oo

The soul—that committee of conniving old men—
is bathed in the spectrum's stairway:
With ultraviolet interests and infrared motives,
it sits an amalgam, separated by space,
marked out in terrestrial latitude and longitude.

White light floods the nerves,
which are subterranean, an unused voice enveloped
in flesh: the hospital, a field of snow
where children heal slowly—some not at all—under the bluish
light that is the sun through the windows of the corridor.

Nerve's motivations are personal: like father, he believes
that something human must be sacrificed to regain
what he has lost. Who is sacrificed does not matter.

oo

In the midst of a conflagration of daughters
father and his unclaimed son collapse fallen stars
into a galaxy of unfiltered expectation. Other sons
revolve centerless—

      Did mother escape only to become her daughter?
      Coaxed endlessly into birth, she's a white shadow of herself—
         albino haired, red eyed.

      Another mother has become a machine.
      has left post-its all over her metallic
      interior—they undo her riddles, solve the distance of time.
         Her daughter flicks open a compartment
         in the tunnel of her core with a screwdriver.

      —I never liked my mother, she says.

oo

The moon is imperfect,
its exploded self
dumped on the earth, which has become desert.
Imagined a portal, it collapsed.

What was Tokyo is now a lake,
its bottom cup-shaped. Buildings assert themselves
fruitlessly: the statue of a winged creature bathes forlornly.
Waves lap on the shore.

The light that serves to interrogate him is spherical,
purple—like the contaminated earth.

What is the child now? A breastplate, an art nouveau vase?
His naked figure goes out of focus.
Even blurred he retains a border though he'd
rather not.

Past, present, future realign: snug.

oo

Narrative like time has only one direction,
no matter how you slice and rearrange it—
and that's a problem because at the end of the narrative
what is there? A solution? Closure? The heel of the loaf? Even
a transformative ending lacks appeal: who wants a stone
that turns base metals to gold? A flooded market's never
good for business. You can wax on about gold's innate virtues
but how can you excuse its softness, the malleability of its
clinging atoms … but I've reeled off-topic. What we desire is girdling—
the routine of the bee's abdominal stripes, within
which change or mutation hurtles in inconclusive odds,
absolving inevitability. Or death, if you prefer. Go ahead, sink
into the retort's murky chemicals, seek the childhood
morass of merging with mother, wipe clean the slate of your identity.

oo

Is this the danger of replication:
that the loved one never dies?
These many copies are not the same, although you may not see it,
mackled at the edges, color sliding thick over surfaces,
between collections of tangible or isolated objects,
lacking the definition of the original;
each copy degraded some undefined percent.
Or is it that the lover is left suspended,
knowing that some unutterable quality is gone:
That the mind, or was it the soul, has gone
elsewhere, if anywhere, and that waiting
is all that remains to the lover, waiting
until the body embrangled with memory
finally crumbles beyond recognition

oo

It is not the words I understand but the voices I remember:

wave lapping over harmonic wave, the beginning gathered,

sprung

∞

What separates us from angels is a field of absolute terror.

Trudging through albino space, ice underfoot, mist above and around—
branches rise out of the white here and there—

not, though, through the icy expanse of the page—

I'm trying to change viewpoints here, to experience more than
what bumps up against the interface of skin and sense: I know what I feel
and I imagine I know what you feel: my eyes float behind yours—
what else is there? Are there boundless sides to this coin? I'm counting on it,
though so far I haven't found the key to the room.

What do you fear?
The question keeps coming up.

Skin curls, retreats: outside becomes inside by means of journey: just as easily
lip turns tongue, glistening orb becomes impulse: light   dark
panoplies of many-armed avatars, pelts of every shade,
promise to lead us beyond the spinning coin, though each stands stranded
in its own monochromatic pitch.

I have been here before—in this world.
I can only try again

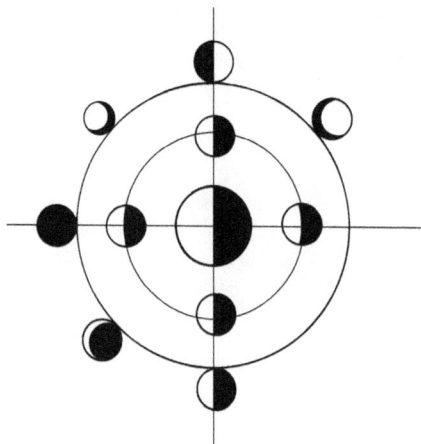

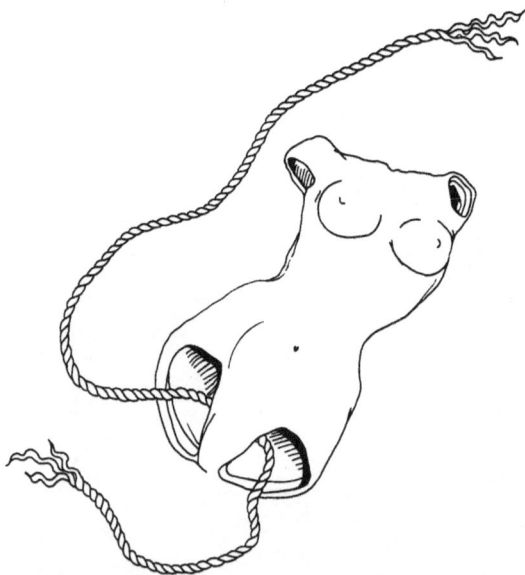

OOOOOOO11

color

Longing is a current
into which he sinks. He surfaces, bobs along.
Fish, like dogs, are everywhere.

Scaly, scintillating, variable—
from their phosphorescent globes,

fish

circle

peer

one-eyed

at

dog, which is always the same
dog

repeating, echoing some animate want,

two-eyed and binocular:

Spinning an aqueous marine sphere—

oo

The doll's eye is also blue
and like a fish's
scintillates along
its iris edge

    A spark:

        drops through aquatic blue

        splashes, reeling

        celluloid,
        unrevealed and inflammable—

           the mouth opens to form an unblinking vowel,
           round O

           pointed A

           looped e

the intersection of tire tracks left by a car turning

       in the newly snowed road, written in the thin
                         crunched ice.

               Within the black dot of pupil

       the lens

       narrows

oo

                    A voice
                    repeats, *M'aidez,*
                    m'aidez

emits photons in glowing lines
each vowel and consonant creating a line of a particular length.
They extrude and fade
extrude and fade.

Broken dolls surround us—*m'aidez, m'aidez*—mouths
open slightly as if they were breathing shallowly through them.
Or had just finished speaking, thought suddenly
distracted by an unexpected and puzzling flashback.
Speech tapers off briefly while the mind reorganizes or
simply stops.

Return to procedure, if it exists.

Mirrors

Claimed not an instrument of enlightenment but illusion—
      image skittering across the surface or sinking
      into the silver backing, which
      echoes the body, tracing its substance in distant matte fields
      that are smooth and near featureless. Through space they reflect,

      lose form, cleaving three dimensions into two,
      snuggling gradations of shadow into line
      until all that's left is movement: a man walking through space

      slowly, seeing the same event over and over:
      the bird flying above becomes an oddly formed airplane,
      mechanical, a headless angel, a feathered gull. He subsumes
      flesh into thought and memory
      reflects that the body's beauty aligns itself with mirrors
      and shiny surfaces, pools formed by rain

oo

Through leaves air fragments, sieved and green,
respires into blue corpuscular veins

      sky the inverted dome of the eye
      skin dawn and permeable
      more than a simple weaving, or plaid, color defining warp and woof

Or a ladder with utilitarian ascent and descent figuring
vertical and horizontal coordinates

The tea in the cup swirls, clockwise, the man who has come to find her
cannot read his future in the musical clatter of china

      time loops in the passage of breath through the heart
      yesterday mingling odorless with tomorrow
      present quicksilver and volatile

Clouds would rear back but instead push across the orange sky
molecules massing, separating across currents

The kimono drops to the floor in soft folds

∞

Sounds shuffle: she deals out words one by one.
Is it a trick or does chance play a role?

Vegetation grieves under the hot sun, water's gone renegade
retreated below the earth

abandoning the sky. The edges of cells
struggle for containment. And escape

in breath.

Words flow: she washes her hands under the faucet.
Is the supply endless or does inhibition play a role?

Molecules, excited, layer and break apart, clouds scudder out
from gravity and exit the planet.

The connection is electric.

                    Everything
                    known is felt.

oo

On the other side of the one-way
mirror a man has lost his memory,
replaced with another's:

tears sparkle through the darkened glass.

As she watches, her body:

        reflects in the looking glass

        in windows

        up from rain sheen'd streets

        surface of the river under which she dives—

        her body lifting finally toward its
        burnished image

Across the night dark city
many-limbed doppel-
gängers multiply, whitely
proliferate: become human—
vanish

oo

Unravel the window—
Beginning with the gleam of sunlight there
in the corner
near the wood frame

Pull a single thread of light

The clear barrier thickens. Air from
outside falters

unfolds like a letter,

                                     falls in a heap

               as a necklace of beads;

                    her hand curls shut, closed like a loose fist

oo

... pulled into recurrence, gesture drowns itself deep into the
brain, flesh and tissue's memory—love goes under. Repetition
dividing mitochondrial from chaos, from terrors of the
unpredictable—
                    What is the point of having a body,
presenting open terrain and suggesting occult passageways?
For you the observer, something perhaps edible, for him the
artist, a reverie, erotic and subliminal. But for her? A past, a
ticket to the park of humanity. She stepped out of it as easily
as clothing, dropped splotches of her skin and frame, discarded
fluids to sink into the earth's hard surface

oo

He wraps her naked shoulders in clothing, his clothing, which doesn't fit her but somehow shrinks to enfold the surfaces that are her body at the moment. Like the eye that only sees what it is focused on, that is to say the mind's eye, because the lens has no focus, is only a partition, curtained by a shutter, a fringed eyelid. The eye in order to see divides itself, discarding myriad simultaneous events—masked children standing in an urban alley, congested stormheads in fast flight across the sky, careening flocks of birds—enchains itself to the solitary, the composed field, the intersection.

Voice over

"We lay down voices before linear depiction—what we know
of the world and the figures that inhabit it is built of broken
lines not mass: cracked black strokes on white."

"We are not together when we speak to each other: I hear your
words but you are unseen: what you say you said in another
time, which was the past. I was the future. You imagined how
I would say what you knew I would say. What if you were
wrong? Which of us would re-enact?"

"Your musicality weaves in black and white. From a newer
moment I could reach out. Soon though we will merge in
a land of suggestible three-dimensionality. Color will exist
there but the mouths we have become will open and shut like
footprints: oblivious and see-through."

oo

Another pencil draws the line between
the conscious and the unconscious

thin and erasable:

like an exhalation—

oo

Her doll's body is a rope of paper prayers.
Out of its soft trunk limbs sprout and into its emptiness
her spirit takes root.
                    Her eyes are blue,
not the soft overcast of air reaching out infinitely,
but glassy like the wet sea
mirroring sky.

She has moved from memory and mystery
to thought: Her body rock, tree, plain and mountain
animate. Hers is sacred and
immortal.

Trees do not inhabit this floating desert. Only dolls
forsaken when she leaves, abandoning the woody body
again, disappearing into thought less tangible than wind.

The mirroring air

And memory is simply a reflection, glassy,
silvered. The dog also remembers, attaches sound to
something other than sound, it lingers
simply in the air as motion moving molecules
but instead is sound plus something remembered

as in expected but perhaps insubstantial,
watery: in a medium other than the flesh that wraps
the bones configured in a chair, the envelope
enclosing the inanimate.

                    It was the soul we were talking
about, not remembering but feeling.
Experience being the mirror we hold under
the nostril—the mist of breath clouding
its clear surface

∞

Along the northern frontier

fog nestles into the earth

Only a third of the people here move, the others remain frozen—

and flocks of birds rise and fall,   their cries

Falling debris

His present is the same color as his past—gray; rain filled,
memory's wilderness a seepage. Half-opened roses above and
below—soaked, shattered, but brightly red. He falls through
the rose-shaped window and into another time he believes is
in the past but persistent always in the moment: mercury from
a broken thermometer skitters in planetary pellets. It's a long
way down, the past transmutes to ochre. He is tweening from
point A to point B: only the ground grows closer in those few
seconds, stretched out, elastic. Sex hooks him into the past.
The falling debris reflected in his eyes flutters like an intimate
note torn in pieces and dropped out the window. When he
wakes color will have returned to the world, but his memory
will liquefy to mizzle. Just walk into a dark room with a candle
to see what I mean.

oo

Sound threads through a labyrinth,
gull's cry, an ear. Sonneteer sound clustered,
metaphor excised—A = B, rather than A,
and B equals C, in turn equaling X. Meant to be binary the impulse
turns into multitudes of sequence. Again she falls simultaneously out
of the brain, fully grown and armored in invisibility.

Morphs into Hong Kong—cluttered, gargantuan, alleys promising
motion revealing nowhere, dead-ending—a music box parading metal
discs, pierced and in step with a metal comb,
the orbital passage of bodies through space:

his mind remembering—

tinkling jangle
abrupt silence

oo

What is (wanted to be done) is understood:
There is only the doing
between the thought and the act. Difficulty
revealing how much want in the doing—

What in that entire room will remain
except
light on a page: a bloom

TEXT NOTES

Anime, Animus, Anima is formed out of many influences but mostly from the imagery from four classic Japanese anime. Parts One and Three—Black and Color—evolved from *Ghost in the Shell* (1995, Production I.G.), an adaptation of the manga of the same name by Masamune Shirow, directed by Mamoru Oshii and written by Kazunori Ito, and *Innocence: Ghost in the Shell 2* (2004, Production I.G. and Studio Ghibli), written and directed by Mamoru Oshii. Part Two—White—evolved from imagery in *Neon Genesis Evangelion* (1995, Gainax), both the television series and the movies, written and directed by Hideaki Anno. Imagery from *Cowboy Bebop* (1998), the Japanese animated television series directed by Shinichiro Watanabe and written by Keiko Nobumoto, appears throughout all three sections.

My fascination with Japanese anime began with my mother's deep love of Japanese culture in general and the graphic art of *ukiyo-e* in particular and was continued by my stepson Emmanuel's passionate love for manga and anime as a young boy. I thank them, most of all, for their love.

I also give thanks to the friends who read the manuscript, including Susanne Dyckman, Todd Melicker, and especially to Paul Hoover and Elizabeth Robinson for their support and appreciation and to Brian Teare for his insightful reading. And finally, I thank Tony Frazer for honoring the work by publishing it.

ACKNOWLEDGEMENTS

Poems from this manuscript have appeared in the following magazines. The author thanks the editors for their kindness and support.

Conjunctions: As "The Clone Poems," which included [A girl enters an elevator ...], [(the imagination of free will ...], [Is this the danger of replication: ...], "Mirrors," [On the other side ...], [Unravel the window ...], [... pulled into recurrence ...], [He wraps her naked shoulders ...].

Switchback: [a stitch in time] and *Falling debris*

www.ingramcontent.com/pod-product-compliance
Lightning Source LLC
Chambersburg PA
CBHW031931080426
42734CB00007B/634